How Can I Serve My Church?

Church Questions

How Can I Serve My Church?

Matthew Emadi

WHEATON, ILLINOIS

Trade paperback ISBN: 978-1-4335-7211-1
ePub ISBN: 978-1-4335-7214-2
PDF ISBN: 978-1-4335-7212-8
Mobipocket ISBN: 978-1-4335-7213-5

Library of Congress Cataloging-in-Publication Data

Names: Emadi, Matthew, 1984- author.
Title: How can I serve my church? / Matthew Emadi.
Description: Wheaton, Il : Crossway, [2021] | Series: Church questions | Includes bibliographical references and index.
Identifiers: LCCN 2020041327 (print) | LCCN 2020041328 (ebook) | ISBN 9781433572111 (trade paperback) | ISBN 9781433572128 (pdf) | ISBN 9781433572135 (mobipocket) | ISBN 9781433572142 (epub)
Subjects: LCSH: Service (Theology) | Church work.
Classification: LCC BT738.4 .E64 2021 (print) | LCC BT738.4 (ebook) | DDC 253—dc23
LC record available at https://lccn.loc.gov/2020041327
LC ebook record available at https://lccn.loc.gov/2020041328

Crossway is a publishing ministry of Good News Publishers.

BP		30	29	28	27	26	25	24	23	22	21
15	14	13	12	11	10	9	8	7	6	5	4	3	2	1

But it shall not be so among you. But whoever would be great among you must be your servant, and whoever would be first among you must be slave of all. For even the Son of Man came not to be served but to serve, and to give his life as a ransom for many.

Mark 10:43–45

Basketball practice had just ended, and Jason lingered until he had my attention.[1] Before he'd said a word, I knew what to expect.

"Hey coach, I think I might quit the team. I'm not really needed."

Jason hardly ever got off the bench, and so he thought that without a meaningful contribution on game days, he served no purpose.

Jason was wrong.

He *did* have a purpose on the team—and a vital one at that, even if he didn't realize it. He came to practice every day. He made his teammates better. Without his presence, everyone would have suffered. He made first-string players work harder. His friendship and camaraderie encouraged his teammates to persevere. Even on game days, he cheered his teammates on.

He was essential to the team whether he realized it or not.

Let me tell you a similar story. Sandy is a member of our local church. She told me one day, "I'm struggling to know what my role is in the church." Sandy didn't lead a ministry. She wasn't responsible for any programs or events. And so she just didn't know what to do. Like Jason, Sandy thought she wasn't getting in when it mattered. She thought she wasn't serving the church.

And also like Jason, she was wrong.

Sandy faithfully shows up every Sunday. She comes early and stays late so that she has plenty of time to talk to others. She's always at members meetings, so she can vote on important issues and ask meaningful questions.

She serves in the nursery and regularly invites church members to her home. She encourages our members with Scripture. She prays for them. She talks to visitors.

In so many ways, Sandy serves our church faithfully and meaningfully. She's vital, despite not having an official title or formal ministry position.

Maybe you're reading this book because you feel the same way. You want to serve your church, but you just don't know what to do. Maybe you're a new Christian, and you don't think you're ready to serve. Maybe you're serving in ways that leave you tired and burnt out, but you don't want to admit it. Maybe you're waiting for some official role in the church or for the pastor to assign you a ministry, and you don't know what to do in the meantime. Maybe you've avoided service because you don't know your calling or how to identify your spiritual gifts.

Wherever you're at, if you're thinking about what faithfulness looks like in serving your local church, then this book is for you.

Small Business Staff or Citizens, Soldiers, and Sons?

Is the Church a Business?

Misconceptions about *serving* the church often stem from misconceptions about *defining* the church. Many people view local churches like small businesses where the pastor is the CEO and the people are the customers. They think the church exists to give them and their children a menu of programs, activities, and events. Those who decide to serve are like employees of the business, making sure the programs are well-organized, the coffee is hot, the marketing is catchy, the activities are plentiful, and the bathrooms are squeaky clean.

Don't misunderstand me—there's nothing wrong with clean bathrooms or hot coffee. In fact, serving your church might mean volunteering to clean the bathrooms or change the coffee filters. But how we think about the church will affect how we think about our service in the church. If we think of local churches as businesses, pastors as CEOs, and churchgoers as consumers, then we will think about service as if we are employees (church members) waiting for the boss (pastor) to give us an assignment (ministry) with a job title—secretly hoping it's not "Director of Bathroom Sanitation."

To think well about service, we need to think biblically about the church. Simply put, local churches aren't like businesses; they're more like embassies of a great kingdom or a family in the same household.

Embassy of the Kingdom of Heaven

On a mission trip, I had the privilege of staying at a Haitian orphanage located across the street from the American embassy. I have to admit that seeing the embassy always provided me a sense of comfort. I knew the embassy represented my government. Even though I was in a foreign country, I could go to the embassy, and they would recognize my citizenship and offer me the protection and privileges that are mine as a citizen.

As Christians, we are citizens of the kingdom of heaven and local churches on earth are little embassies of that kingdom. In other words, they represent heaven on earth (Matt. 16:18–19; Eph. 2:19; Phil. 3:20). Jesus Christ is the king of heaven's kingdom, and he rules his church through his word—the Bible (Eph. 1:19–23). Through church membership, discipline, and baptism, the Lord's local churches identify Christians on earth. They speak on behalf of heaven to declare to the world *who is* and *who is not* a citizen of Christ's kingdom (Matt. 18:15–20).

What does any of this have to do with how we think about serving our church? Everything! First, we should recognize that all of our service is ultimately done for the glory of our great King, the Lord Jesus Christ. Not only did he give up his own life to pay the penalty for our sins and reconcile us to God, he also gives us the amazing privilege of serving him. Imagine that! Every ministry, no matter how small or hidden from the world, is meaningful when done for the glory of Christ. Even a cup of cold water given to his people will not go unnoticed by King Jesus (Matt. 10:42). He sees, he knows, and he will one day say to people who labored for him in total obscurity, "Well done, good and faithful servant" (Matt. 25:23). By far one of the greatest privileges of our lives is that we get to serve the King of kings by serving the people he loves.

Second, seeing the church as an embassy of Christ's kingdom reminds us we are not employees of a business, casually checking off a daily to-do list. We are citizens, soldiers even, of an otherworldly kingdom in hostile territory (Eph. 6:11; 2 Tim. 2:3–5). We belong to heaven, even as we live in a foreign land under the sway of an evil spiritual ruler named Satan (John 12:31; 2 Cor. 4:4; Eph. 2:2). We once lived under his tyranny as enemies of God, but through the gospel, we have been transferred out of his domain and into the kingdom of God's beloved Son (Col. 1:13). The apostle Paul's words are just as true for us as they were for the Ephesian Christians:

> For we do not wrestle against flesh and blood, but against the rulers, against the authorities, against the cosmic powers over this present darkness, against the

spiritual forces of evil in the heavenly places. (Eph. 6:12)

The stakes are high, and we have work to do. When we disciple a new Christian, we're not just being friendly; we're preparing them for battle against the world, the flesh, and the devil (Eph. 3:13–14). When we gather for corporate worship on the Lord's Day, we're not just doing our duty; we're displaying the manifold wisdom of God to the rulers and authorities in the heavenly places (Eph. 3:10). When we take part in missions and evangelism, we're not peddling a product; we're announcing to the world that all authority in heaven and on earth belongs to Christ, and Satan can no longer deceive the nations (Matt. 28:18–20; Col. 2:15).

During World War II, ordinary American citizens rationed consumer goods, recycled materials, and kept factories running night and day. They sacrificed much because they knew the stakes. Do we? Do we realize that we are citizens of Christ's kingdom? Do we realize our churches are outposts of that kingdom on the front lines of a spiritual battle? Refusing to serve the church would be like a soldier pulling up a chair to sip Kool-Aid while he watches his comrades fight the war.

The stakes are high, and the needs are great. For this reason Christ calls every member of his church to enlist in service. Why? Because a local church is an embassy of Christ's kingdom.

The Household of God

A local church is also a family. Paul told Timothy that the "church of the living God" is the "household of God" (Eph. 2:19; 1 Tim. 3:15). We're not a gathering of strangers, acquaintances, or colleagues; we're brothers and sisters in Christ. We've been adopted as sons and daughters into the family of God.

Before the foundation of the world, God the Father predestined us in love for adoption (Eph. 1:5). He sent the eternal Son of God, the second person of the Trinity, to become a man and die on a cross as our substitute for the forgiveness of our sins (Eph. 1:7). And though we were once hopeless, alienated from God, separated from Christ, and dead in our trespasses and sins, the Father and the Son sent the Holy Spirit to make us alive together with Christ (Eph. 2:1–6, 11–13). And now, the Spirit of Christ dwells in our hearts so that we cry out "Abba, Father" (Rom. 8:15). What manner of love the Father has given to us that we should be called children of God (1 John 3:1)!

No matter how diverse the individual members of a local church might be, the gospel of Jesus Christ has made us children of God (John 1:12; Gal. 3:26). We are members of the same household, indwelt by the same Spirit, we have access to the same Father (Eph. 2:18–19), and we fellowship around the same table (1 Cor. 11:23–26).

How should this view of church affect our view of service?

At the very least, it should orient much of our service toward relationships and free us to start serving others in meaningful ways without official "ministry positions," "callings," or "titles." Think about your biological family for a minute.

Do you need to organize a cleaning program before you do the dishes? Do you need a title like "activity coordinator" before you take the kids to the park? Do you need to feel "called" to teach before you lead your family in spiritual devotions? Do you need to organize a discipleship program before you talk to your kids about Christian character?

Of course not.

You serve your biological family in hundreds of ways because you love them, you're committed to them, and you value those relationships. If you're a parent, you probably prioritize time with your children. If you're a spouse, you probably invest in your relationship with your husband or wife, or at least you should. If you're a single college student, you probably make an intentional effort to call your parents. In so many ways, you actively, intentionally, and even intuitively serve your family. This type of service should characterize how we engage with others in our local church.

I see this type of selfless, family-like service in my own congregation. When Mandy had a baby, Alyssa organized a meal schedule for Mandy's family, even though she doesn't have a formal position at the church. John and Euna regularly have singles over for dinner and take members of our youth group to lunch on Sunday afternoons. Mark and Nancy host a Bible study in their living room on Thursday evenings. Eric goes out of his way every Sunday to make visitors feel welcome. Barbara keeps tabs on some of our older members and often drives them to doctor appointments. Mark fills the water dispenser every Sunday morning even though nobody has ever asked him to. Brittany practices hospitality, regularly inviting church members into her home.

None of these church members have official ministry titles, and none of these activities are part of a church program. They simply recognize they're part of a family, so they act like members of a family.

As part of Christ's church, God has given us a spiritual family that will endure into eternity. The hallmark of God's family is love for God and love for one another. So how are you loving

God and his people? How are you serving them? Are you ready to prioritize those relationships and make sacrifices in your schedule to serve your brothers and sisters in meaningful ways? Are you ready to serve alongside them to see Christ's kingdom expand beyond the walls of your own church?

I hope so.

Now for the tricky part: What does that look like? Hopefully you're already thinking of ways you can serve Christ by serving his people. If not, that's okay. In the next section, I'll describe four practical ways that all of us can serve our church.

Four Meaningful Ways to Serve Your Church

Christians, Assemble!

I have six children, five boys and one girl. As you can probably imagine, my boys love superheroes—and okay, maybe I do too. Among our favorites are *The Avengers*. My two oldest boys often come with me to the local library on Saturday afternoons so they can read books about the adventures of Captain America, Ironman, the Incredible Hulk, and Thor while I finish preparing my sermon. Each Avenger has unique gifts and strengths, but none of them is powerful enough to defeat mighty Thanos and his army alone. They need each other. Isolated they fail. But together, their combined strength is an unstoppable force. Their iconic call reflects this: "Avengers, Assemble!"

As Christians, the most fundamental act of service is to assemble with God's people for corporate worship on the Lord's Day. Maybe you're thinking, "How is showing up on Sunday an act of service? Isn't that setting the bar too low?" Not if we think biblically about what happens in our church gatherings.

Consider what that author of Hebrews said:

And let us consider how to stir up one another to love and good works, not neglecting to meet together, as is the habit of some, but encouraging one another, and all

the more as you see the Day drawing near.
(Hebrews 10:24–25)

How do Christians stir each other up to love and good works? How do they encourage each other to persevere in the faith? By not neglecting to meet together! Or to put it positively: *we stir each other up to love and encourage each other by assembling.* Your mere presence at your church's corporate gathering on the Lord's Day serves your church.

We don't typically think about our presence in the assembly as an act of service, but think about it for a moment. Our lives are full of discouragements and adversity. The world constantly bombards us with ungodly ideologies that want to lure us away from the truth. Satan is like a roaring lion seeking to devour us with lies, condemnation, and temptations. He desperately wants to snuff out our faith or make us entirely ineffective for kingdom work. We so often feel alone and isolated—in our schools, workplaces, and communities. Sometimes, if we're honest, we even begin to question our beliefs. It seems like the whole world is against us.

God knows this. And so he has given us one day every week to gather with other believers for encouragement. In each other's presence, we give and receive encouragement by reminding one another we're not alone. We assemble with Christians from all different walks of life to testify to one another that Christ is king, God's word is true, and his church will prevail until Christ comes again. Our assembly is our corporate stand against the rulers, authorities, and cosmic powers of this present darkness. Together, we who share the same Spirit and are united in love and truth display the manifold wisdom of God to the rulers and authorities in the heavenly places (Eph. 3:10).

I don't know about you, but I need that kind of encouragement. I need others to point me back to the Bible. I need others to model love and faithfulness to Christ, and to remind me that I'm not following Jesus alone.

You might lead five different ministries. You might be the first to volunteer for workdays and programs. But if you don't prioritize the corporate gathering, then you're doing a great *disservice* both to the church and yourself. If Christians do not heed the call to assemble, then an opportunity for great encouragement actually becomes a moment of great discouragement.

Consider how not regularly attending your church affects others. Imagine you're on a basketball team with twelve players. You can't wait for the season to start. Excitedly, you show up to practice the first day . . . and only eight players are there. *Where is everyone?* you wonder.

Day two of practice rolls around. This time, there are only six players present—some from day one, some not. Day three, five players; day four, seven players. Over time, you start to notice a pattern. The players on the team really don't care that much about the team.

Finally, it's game day. But even *then*, only five players show up. Your team must have five players on the court the whole time, so you have to play the whole game. No substitutions, no breaks, no players cheering the team on from the bench. For the second game, only three players show up; you forfeit.

If this pattern continued, would you be encouraged or discouraged? Pretty easy answer, right? You would be frustrated, discouraged, and maybe even a little hurt. You might even think about quitting the team.

Now imagine if you have a church full of people who don't prioritize corporate worship on the Lord's Day. Imagine if half the church is missing every single Sunday. Do you see why gathering *with* the church is a great service *to* the church?

So Christians, assemble! Prioritize the Lord's Day gathering. Your presence serves your church.

But don't stop there. You have a great opportunity to serve your church at your assembly by focusing on other people. What does that look like? Here are some ideas:

- Consider arriving early just to chat with people. Introduce yourself to strangers.
- Step out of your comfort zone and welcome visitors. It might be their first time in a Christian church.

- Consider serving on a regular basis in the nursery or children's ministry during corporate worship.
- Sing loudly and cheerfully for the glory of God and for the good of the whole church. The apostle Paul tells us that we teach and admonish one another in all wisdom when we sing psalms, hymns, and spiritual songs (Col. 3:16).
- Sit by different people, or invite a single person to sit with you.
- Don't rush out the door after the service! Hang around and talk to people. Ask them about the sermon. What did they learn? How were they impacted? Ask them how you can pray for them during the week.

Christians assemble. That's what we do. Don't underestimate the significance of your presence with God's people. Prioritize corporate worship on the Lord's Day, and make every effort to assemble with the church for other reasons as well. Attend members meetings and prayer services. Stir up your fellow believers to love and good works, and encourage them to persevere to the end.

Hospitality from a Coconut Tree

I never knew hospitality could be so dangerous. I was in Cap Rouge, Haiti, admiring the beauty of the tropical landscape when our host signaled to a young Haitian man and muttered something in Creole. The young man strapped on a machete and walked barefoot over to the base of a coconut tree which stood approximately 50 feet tall. He looked up, crossed himself, and then grabbed hold of the tree and started climbing.

In both amazement and terror, I watched as this young man shimmied up the tree without a single branch to grasp for support or safety. I knew why he was climbing: to retrieve fresh coconuts for us. As he climbed higher and higher, I could hardly watch. One slip and he might plummet to his death. My anxiety grew as I repeated the words in my mind: *Please don't fall, please don't fall, please don't fall. I don't need the coconut. Please stop! I feel loved already! Just come back down!*

Eventually, he made it to the top, cut down a few coconuts, and gave them to us. I had more coconut juice than I ever wanted.

To this day, I consider that young man's act of hospitality one of the nicest things anyone has ever done for me. He didn't just stroll down to the grocery store to pick up some coconut juice. He exerted great effort and even risked his life for me, a stranger. We sat there drinking our coconut juice while he dripped with sweat from a feat that made America Ninja Warrior look like child's play.

I learned a lesson that day. Hospitality requires self-giving, which means it requires sacrifice, energy, and loving people more than possessions.

Our churches should be characterized by this kind of hospitality. Put another way, our churches should be like the early church:

And all who believed were together and had all things in common. And they were selling their possessions and belongings and distributing the proceeds to all, as any had need. And day by day, attending the temple together and breaking bread in their homes, they received their food with glad and generous hearts, praising God and having favor with all the people. And the Lord added to their number day by day those who were being saved. (Acts 2:44–47)

Notice that Luke says they were "together" (v. 44), and day by day, they broke bread in their homes (v. 46). Like a family, they came together, showing regular hospitality to each other.

Strangely, hospitality receives so little emphasis in many of our churches. When is the last time you heard a sermon or Sunday school lesson on hospitality? When is the last time someone encouraged you to serve your church by practicing hospitality? Yet the Bible regularly depicts hospitality as the kind of work that God's people should embrace:

- Job welcomed the sojourner and opened his door to the traveler (Job 31:32).
- God, through Isaiah, reminded the people of Israel that true worship meant sharing their bread with the hungry and bringing the homeless into their houses (Isa. 58:7).

- Jesus said, "But when you give a feast, invite the poor, the crippled, the lame, the blind, and you will be blessed, because they cannot repay you" (Luke 14:13–14).
- Paul instructed Christians to "contribute to the needs of the saints and seek to show hospitality" (Rom. 12:13).
- The author of Hebrews told his readers not to "neglect to show hospitality to strangers" (Heb. 13:2).
- Peter said, "Show hospitality to one another without grumbling" (1 Pet. 4:9).
- Even one of the essential qualifications for the pastoral office is that pastors must be hospitable (Titus 1:8).

So how can you serve your church? Practice hospitality. Build time into your schedule to invite church members and lost neighbors into your home—maybe for dinner, coffee, or just to spend time together. Encourage them, pray for them, serve them, share their joys and their burdens. Also, accept invitations so others can show you hospitality. Open up your home to visiting missionaries. Take in another couple's children and feed them, so their mom and dad can go on a date. Welcome unbelievers into your house; yours might be the only Christian home they've ever entered.

We shouldn't use our homes as bunkers where we retreat from people and their problems but, in the words of Rosaria Butterfield, as "hospitals, embassies, and incubators" where we receive the lonely, weary, and wounded with compassion.[2] We should be willing to step out of our comfort zone and welcome strangers and people very different than us. Did you know that almost all of the famous "one another" passages in the New Testament can be practiced from your living room (cf. Rom. 12:10; 14:19; Gal. 6:2; Eph. 4:32; Col. 3:13)?

Practicing hospitality is costly. It will affect your budget, eat up your schedule, and expend your physical and emotional energy. It may even mean your stuff gets ruined. On more than one occasion, guests left us with damaged walls, ruined flower beds, broken furniture, pee on the carpets (children can be messier than pets!), and even sand in my bed. But it's all worth it. Why? Because hospitality is about service, and service requires sacrifice and self-giving.

It's so easy to ignore all this. That's why the author of Hebrews tells us, "Do not neglect to show hospitality" (Heb. 13:2; see also, Rom. 12:13; 1 Pet. 4:9). I get it; everyone is busy. We have jobs to perform, families to feed, soccer games to attend, emails to ignore, vacations to plan, lawns to mow, laundry to avoid, bills to pay, and diapers to beg your spouse to change. We're all busy. But this should push us toward intentionality not inaction. We need to build time into our schedule to practice hospitality. If we don't, it will get neglected.

Where can we find lasting motivation for this? What will compel us to sacrifice our time, energy, and resources? Surely the story of the man who climbed the tree is enough to inspire us all. I'm not referring to the young man in Haiti, though I'll never forget him. I'm talking about Jesus. Jesus didn't just risk his life. He gave up his life for us by ascending Calvary's tree. Through his sacrifice, he has brought strangers into his household and seated us around his table (1 Cor. 11:23–26; Eph. 2:19). Freely we've received, now freely we ought to give—of ourselves, our food, our stuff, our time, and our affection, all for the sake of others.

The Gospel Is a Snow-Capped Mountain?

I asked a police chaplain at lunch, "What is the gospel?"

"The gospel is about God's love," he answered.

"How does God manifest his love in the gospel?"

"God's love is a snow-capped mountain," he said.

I nearly choked on my organic, longevity-of-life-increasing pasta. "A snow-capped mountain? Did you say the gospel is a message about God's love revealed in a snow-capped mountain?" Sadly, this was, in fact, how the chaplain explained the gospel.

People need to hear the biblical gospel. They need to hear about God's love revealed in Jesus Christ, God the Son incarnate. I shared with the chaplain that Jesus was crucified under the wrath of God to pay the penalty for sin. He substituted himself in the place of sinners, bearing their condemnation and reconciling them to God. He then rose from the grave on the third day, conquering sin and death. And now by God's grace alone, we can be right with God through faith alone in Jesus Christ alone.

People need the gospel. As Christians, we have the privilege of serving Christ and his church by making the gospel known. In doing so, we do our part in fulfilling the mission of the church. Jesus tells us in Matthew 28:18–20:

> And Jesus came and said to them, "All authority in heaven and on earth has been given to me. Go therefore and make disciples of all nations, baptizing them in the name of the Father and of the Son and of the Holy Spirit, teaching them to observe all that I have commanded you. And behold, I am with you always, to the end of the age."

Our mission is clear: We are to make disciples. This will include helping Christians learn the Bible and what it means to obey Christ (more on this below). This will also include telling the gospel to unbelievers and calling them to repent of their sin and to trust in Christ.

Here's the simple truth: You don't need an evangelistic program to start sharing the gospel. You have friends, family members, neighbors, coworkers, and acquaintances who need to hear it. You might ask, "What if I'm not gifted in evangelism?" That's okay. Most Christians don't feel "gifted" in evangelism. The good news is that "gifting" is not a prerequisite for taking part in the mission. Jesus has given the Great Commission to every Christian, and our participation is one way we serve our Lord.

Of course we can improve in our evangelistic ability. But the best way to improve is to practice. The more you share the gospel, the better you'll become. You might also consider reading some books on personal evangelism like Isaac Adams's *What If I'm Discouraged in My Evangelism?* or Mark Dever's *The Gospel and Personal Evangelism*.[3]

It is worth saying again: we serve our church by taking part in the mission of the church.

Let me tell you a story about a man named James with a traveling evangelism ministry. James is a member of our church. He loves our church and serves our church by sharing the gospel regularly with others. He doesn't lead an evangelistic ministry, but he has an evangelistic ministry. What is it? Delivering furniture.

Everywhere James goes to deliver furniture, he tells people about Jesus. In fact, he even painted big red letters on the side of his delivery van: "Amen Delivery Services. Ask Me About My Church." Yes, his cell phone number is on the side of the van as well. Why does he want people to ask him about his church? Because he knows he can invite unbelievers there to hear the gospel and rub shoulders with other Christians. James serves his church by sharing the gospel regularly.

You don't need to wait around for an evangelistic program. In fact, you *shouldn't* do that. Instead, ask God to help you see the opportunities all around you. You will serve your church well when you take part in your church's mission.

Teach Us to Pummel!

"First, elbow me in the stomach. Second, flip me over your hip and slam me onto the ground."

"Like this?"

"Yes, great! I really felt that. Now do it faster and harder."

These are the kinds of morbid conversations I loved having with my martial arts instructor (we called him *Sensei*) during my senior year in college. I signed up for a karate class as an elective, but it was not my first attempt at karate. My dad was a martial arts instructor, so I had been studying karate since I was five years old. When my college sensei found out I had a black belt in a Japanese style of martial arts, he asked me to teach him. So that's what I did. I went to class early every week to train him. When students began arriving for class, I would put on a white belt, take my place among the students, and listen to his instruction.

My college sensei and I mutually benefited from our relationship because we were both willing to give and receive instruction. We were *discipling* each other in the martial arts.

Discipling in the church works similarly. No, I'm not suggesting you put sister Jane in an arm bar at the next potluck. I simply mean that discipleship happens when we are willing to give and receive instruction from other believers. Remember, Jesus gave us a mission to make disciples (Matt. 28:18–20). That means we not only share the gospel with unbelievers; we also teach Christians what it looks like to follow Christ. Making disciples involves helping other Christians learn how to become more like Christ.

Discipling others is one of the most important ways you can serve your church. Why do I say that? Because Christians still sin. We're prone to wander. We have blind spots. False doctrine is rampant and easily accessible. Biblical illiteracy is high. False teachers abound. Spiritual warfare is real. The world is attractive. Sacrifice is hard. And we're often set in our ways. Christians need other Christians to help them faithfully follow Jesus amid so many dangers, toils, and snares.

In 2018, Ligonier Ministries polled American evangelicals about basic and essential Christian doctrines.[4] The results were alarming.

- 52 percent of American evangelicals believe most people are good by nature.
- 51 percent believe that God accepts the worship of all religions including Christianity, Judaism, and Islam.
- 78 percent agree that Jesus is the first and greatest being created by God.

The majority of professing American evangelicals are wrong about fundamental Christian doctrines. Of those surveyed, 78 percent endorse an ancient heretical view of Jesus that more closely represents modern-day Mormonism, not biblical Christianity. At the very least, such statistics reveal the need for meaningful discipling.

The apostle Paul told the Ephesians that they were to "grow up" in Christ into "mature manhood" (Eph. 4:13–15). They were not to be like children tossed around by every wind of doctrine and captive to human cunning and deception (Eph. 4:14). Instead, they were to speak the truth in love so that the whole body would build itself up in love (Eph. 4:15–16).

Speaking the truth in love is how we disciple one another. As church members speak and apply sound doctrine to each other, the whole church becomes more like Jesus. In Paul's words, they grow up in every way into Christ (Eph. 4:15).

What might this look like in the life of a church? Here are some ideas:

- If you're an older woman, spend time with younger women. Use Titus 2:3–5 as a guide.
- Ask your pastor if there is a new believer who needs discipling. Take a few months (or a few years!) and invest in that person. Read the Bible and great Christian books together.
- Are you a new believer? Ask a mature Christian to disciple you. I'm sure he or she will have some ideas of what that could look like.
- Find one other person in the church to meet with weekly or monthly for prayer and Bible study. Perhaps you'll both be discipling each other since you'll both benefit from the relationship.
- Ask your pastor if you can accompany him on some of his pastoral visits or review his sermons with him.

- If you lead a small group or teach a Sunday school class to children or adults, identify someone to replace you. Show them how you prepare to teach and give them guidance on how to teach others.
- Teach by example. Invite others into your home and model Christian maturity for them. For instance, invite fellow Christians to observe how you parent or how you treat your spouse.

If church members don't disciple each other, then the whole church will suffer. Pastors can't disciple everyone individually. They need your participation in the work of ministry (Eph. 4:11–12). You don't need to lead a church-sponsored Bible study or teach a Sunday school class to disciple others. Start with one person and help them follow Jesus with you.

What about My Spiritual Gifts?

I'm near the end of a book about service, and I've said nothing about spiritual gifts. Shouldn't a book like this *begin* with a discussion of spiritual gifts? Not necessarily. Don't get me wrong—spiritual gifts are important. The Lord Jesus Christ gifts his people for service (1 Cor. 12:1–11). But many Christians wrongly think they must be gifted in a specific area before they can commit to serving. Have you ever heard someone say something like:

- "Toddlers scare me. I'm just not gifted with children."
- "Hospitality is great, but God hasn't called me to that because my house isn't big enough."
- "God just hasn't given me a heart for youth ministry."
- "I'm all for evangelism, I'm just not gifted."

Maybe you've said something similar. But spiritual gifts aren't meant to restrict us from serving the body. They're for the body's common good (1 Cor. 12:7). Neither are they to function as excuses for why we can't serve in ways that make us feel uncomfortable. Kevin Yi says it well:

> Rather than using the idea of "calling" and "gifts" to make excuses for why we can't serve a subset of church members, we should be

exhorting one another to take risks in loving and serving others even when it stretches us outside of our comfort zone.[5]

Comfort, passion, gifting, and confidence aren't prerequisites for service. Weakness and humble desperation for God's help are. I've never once felt gifted or confident in unclogging toilets. It's not my passion. Yet I have done it many times in my house and in the church. Why? Because there was a need.

There are needs in your church. All kinds of them. So stop waiting for the perfect opportunity that "aligns with your gifts." Instead of refraining from service until you figure out your calling or your spiritual gifts, serve in various kinds of ways, and your gifts will surface through your service.

"The Greatest among You Will Be Your Servant"

Jesus and his disciples were on their way to Jerusalem. Jesus knew what awaited him. He was going to suffer and die on a Roman cross.

But the disciples didn't understand. They were preoccupied with something else. They wanted power; they wanted glory. On the way to Golgotha, they argued about who was the greatest (Mark 9:33–37). James and John were even bold enough to ask for the best positions of honor (Mark 10:35–38). They didn't know what they were asking. But there, on the road to Calvary, Jesus told his disciples how they could achieve greatness in his kingdom:

> And Jesus called them to him and said to them, "You know that those who are considered rulers of the Gentiles lord it over them, and their great ones exercise authority over them. But it shall not be so among you. But whoever would be great among you must be your servant, and whoever would be first among you must be slave of all. For even the Son of Man came not to be served but to serve, and to give his life as a ransom for many." (Mark 10:42–45)

Maybe you're reading this book because you're not serving your church, and you know it's time to start. I pray that this book will help you to see the incredible opportunities waiting for you. Don't miss out on the joy of serving the family of God. You belong to that family!

On the other hand, perhaps this book has helped you realize that you've been serving your church in meaningful ways without even realizing it. My encouragement to you is simple: keep doing what you're doing. Don't lose heart in showing hospitality, or meeting with that one person for Bible study, or showing up to church every Lord's Day, or sharing the gospel with others. These acts of service come with no glamour or fanfare, but neither does serving a cup of cold water to one of Jesus's disciples (Matt. 10:42).

One of the ironies of Christian service is that we often do not realize we're doing it when we do it well because Christian service is spectacularly ordinary, un-grandiose, and normal—kind of like serving your family.

This is what Sandy didn't understand. Remember her? I told her story at the beginning. Sandy is the kind of person Jesus said will inherit the kingdom when he returns:

Then the King will say to those on his right,
"Come, you who are blessed by my Father,
inherit the kingdom prepared for you from
the foundation of the world. For I was hungry and you gave me food, I was thirsty and
you gave me drink, I was a stranger and you
welcomed me, I was naked and you clothed
me, I was sick and you visited me, I was in
prison and you came to me." (Matt. 25:34–36)

If, with Sandy, you find yourself wondering
if you've served Christ like that, then you're in
good company. Jesus went on to say,

Then the righteous will answer him, saying, "Lord, when did we see you hungry
and feed you, or thirsty and give you drink?
And when did we see you a stranger and
welcome you, or naked and clothe you?
And when did we see you sick or in prison
and visit you?" And the King will answer
them, "Truly, I say to you, as you did it to
one of the least of these my brothers, you
did it to me." (Matt. 25:37–40)

When we serve Christ's "brothers" in ordinary ways—feeding them, clothing them, showing them hospitality, taking them a meal, and visiting them in their illness—we're serving Christ himself.

May God give us the strength to labor with all of his might to serve the body of Christ (Col. 1:29), remembering that even our Lord Jesus did not come "to be served but to serve, and to give his life as a ransom for many" (Mark 10:45).

Notes

1. Personal stories involving other individuals are shared in this booklet with permission from those individuals. Often pseudonyms have been used for privacy.
2. Rosaria Butterfield, "The Best Weapon Is an Open Door," Desiring God, May 5, 2018, https://www.desiringgod.org /articles/the-best-weapon-is-an-open-door.
3. Isaac Adams, *What If I'm Discouraged in My Evangelism?* Church Questions (Wheaton, IL: Crossway, 2020); or Mark Dever, *The Gospel and Personal Evangelism* (Wheaton, IL: Crossway, 2007).
4. The State of Theology, accessed February 6, 2020, https://thestateoftheology.com.
5. Kevin Yi, "Don't Use 'Calling' to Avoid Serving," The Gospel Coalition, August 17, 2019, https://www.the gospelcoalition.org/article/dont-use-calling-avoid -serving/.

Scripture Index

9Marks

Building Healthy Churches

9Marks exists to equip church leaders with a biblical vision and practical resources for displaying God's glory to the nations through healthy churches.

To that end, we want to see churches characterized by these nine marks of health:

1. Expositional Preaching
2. Gospel Doctrine
3. A Biblical Understanding of Conversion and Evangelism
4. Biblical Church Membership
5. Biblical Church Discipline
6. A Biblical Concern for Discipleship and Growth
7. Biblical Church Leadership
8. A Biblical Understanding of the Practice of Prayer
9. A Biblical Understanding and Practice of Missions

Find all our Crossway titles and other resources at 9Marks.org.

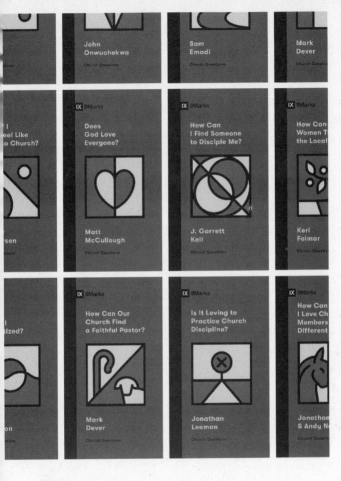

John
Onwuchekwa

Church Questions

Sam
Emadi

Church Questions

Mark
Dever

Church Questions

...el Like
...o Church?

...rsen

...ions

Does
God Love
Everyone?

Matt
McCullough

Church Questions

How Can
I Find Someone
to Disciple Me?

J. Garrett
Kell

Church Questions

How Can
Women T...
the Local...

Keri
Folmar

Church Questions

...
...tized?

...on

...ians

How Can Our
Church Find
a Faithful Pastor?

Mark
Dever

Church Questions

Is It Loving to
Practice Church
Discipline?

Jonathan
Leeman

Church Questions

How Can
I Love Ch...
Members
Different...

Jonathan
& Andy N...

Church Questions

IX 9Marks Church Questions

Providing ordinary Christians with sound and
accessible biblical teaching by answering
common questions about church life.

For more information, visit crossway.org.